IMAGES
of America

THE MARINES AT
TWENTYNINE PALMS

ON THE COVER: The CH-37 Mojave helicopter, shown as troops disembark, was delivered to the Marine Corps in the late 1950s and represented the corps' first heavy-left helicopter.

IMAGES
of America

THE MARINES AT TWENTYNINE PALMS

Thomas Q. O'Hara

ARCADIA
PUBLISHING

Published by Arcadia Publishing
Charleston SC, Chicago IL, Portsmouth NH, San Francisco CA

Printed in the United States of America

Library of Congress Catalog Card Number: 2006931414

For all general information contact Arcadia Publishing at:
Telephone 843-853-2070
Fax 843-853-0044
E-mail sales@arcadiapublishing.com
For customer service and orders:
Toll-Free 1-888-313-2665

Visit us on the Internet at www.arcadiapublishing.com

This book is dedicated to Brig. Gen. Jerry Ward, Lt. Col. Bill Haines, and Gunnery Sergeant Allen Horton. They were truly "three great marines who passed much too early."

CONTENTS

ACKNOWLEDGMENTS

The author would like to thank the Twentynine Palms Historical Society for their assistance. A thanks also goes to George Dietsch for his photograph advice and expertise.

Two sources of images are identified by their acronyms following their first mention. These are the Twentynine Palms Historical Society (TPHS) and the U.S. Marine Corps' Flying Leatherneck Museum at Miramar Air Station (FLAM).

INTRODUCTION

When Captain Fremont, the famous American explorer, first entered the wilderness that became Southern California, he passed near the present-day Twentynine Palms area. He reported to the War Department, "The contents of this great basin are yet to be examined. That it is peopled we know, but miserably and sparsely. From all that I heard and saw I should say that humanity here appears is in its lowest form and in its most elemental state."

The first recorded exploration of the Twentynine Palms area by non–Native American or non-Spanish explorers was made by Col. Henry Washington in 1855. He found people from the Chemchuevi tribe living near a water source they pronounced "Marrah," which means land of little water. The spring or watering hole came to be known as the Oasis of Mara, and as the only reliable watering hole within miles, it served as the basis for the settlement of the area.

When white men stampeded to California in search of gold in the mid-1800s, they avoided the desert areas because there was little water. Eventually the lust for gold spread to the arid terrain, and prospectors found precious metal at Twentynine Palms in 1879. The Oasis of Mara, first mapped in 1855, served as the starting point for prospectors and miners and then anyone coming into the area to build a home or a business. In 1890, an adobe hut was built at the oasis and served as the primary residence for anyone transiting the area. For many years, the adobe withstood the elements, while mining in the area flourished. The Dale Mines yielded over $3 million worth of gold. In the nearby towns of Old Dale and New Dale, saloons and gambling tables, and even dance halls, provided entertainment for local residents. A stagecoach traveled through Twentynine Palms until 1916, when automobiles put it out of business. Shortly after World War I, the mining industry also "panned out."

The source of the name Twentynine Palms has never been authenticated, but stories vary from Colonel Washington finding 29 palm trees around the Oasis of Mara, when he came through the area in 1855, to the account about a survey team who found 26 palm trees in 1858. An early gold mine "claim" identified its location as a given distance from the "Twentynine Palms Spring." Logic would dictate that at one time or another, when any number of English-speaking explorers were present, there were 29 palm trees growing around the Oasis of Mara, and the name caught on.

Over the years, prospecting and gold mining faded into historical context and cattle grazing never really prospered. Homesteading became the local preoccupation. The Homestead Act passed by Congress initially allowed squatters the right to claim 160 acres of land for their personal use. In 1933, it was decreased to five acres known as "jackrabbit homesteads." The opportunity brought thousands of settlers into the area. The saying at the time was that "Uncle Sam bets you 160 acres of sand that you can't live on it for three years without starving to death." In most cases, Uncle Sam was right.

The modern-day essence of Twentynine Palms began to form between the world wars. The Bagleys arrived to open their store, and Dr. James B. Luckie journeyed from Pasadena to use the area's climate as an early health spa to help cure and rehabilitate World War I veterans as well as asthma and arthritis patients. Dr. Luckie was a medical officer during World War I who established a practice in Pasadena, California, after the war. He sent many patients to live in Twentynine Palms to recover from the poison gas injuries suffered during the war. The Plaza Business Center sprung to life and the famous Twentynine Palms City Hall, famously depicted in *Ripley's Believe It or Not*, gave the growing community an identity.

The Twentynine Palms School House was built in 1927 to accommodate the community's eight students, and eventually it served the entire Morongo Basin. Today the schoolhouse is a museum near the Twentynine Palms Inn, where the history and flavor of the community is well preserved and documented.

In 1936, the nearby Joshua Tree National Monument was created, drawing an endless stream of tourists into the area each year. In 1941, an airfield was established five miles outside of Twentynine Palms and called Condor Field. With the advent of World War II, the Army Air Corps arrived in strength and initially used the airfield for training pilots in glider aircraft. In 1944, the U.S. Navy took over the field, using it for general aviation training until the end of World War II. In 1945, the land was transferred to San Bernardino County until the marines arrived to take possession in 1952.

One

OLD AIRFIELD AT TWENTYNINE PALMS

In 1941, war with Japan loomed on the horizon, spawning plans for new military facilities across the nation. Five miles outside Twentynine Palms, Condor Field was constructed, and with the advent of World War II, the Army Air Corps arrived in strength, using the field to train glider pilots. During the early years of World War II, everything involved in the production of aircraft was in short supply. In place of aluminum aircraft, manufacturers used wood, and in the place of engines, they produced gliders. As the nation caught up with wartime demands and resources, gliders were phased out of extensive use.

At its peak, Condor Field was one of the many booming World War II airfields built all over California and the nation by the U.S. Army Air Corps, the forerunner of the U.S. Air Force, as well as the U.S. Navy and the U.S. Marine Corps. Emerging from the Great Depression of the 1930s, those who trained and worked at military airfields during the prewar and war years of the 1940s often appear unnaturally enthusiastic. Military life and life at air stations in particular combined the best and worst of all possibilities. Facilities at air stations were normally far above average. At the time, life was very good indeed for pilots and other personnel prior to their deployment into World War II combat zones.

Condor Field of the early 1940s was a full-service air station with extensive runways, hangars, refueling, and maintenance facilities. Initially, gliders and tow planes filled the skies. But in 1944, the U.S. Navy took over the field for general aviation, which lasted until the end of World War II. In 1945, the land was transferred to San Bernardino County until the marines took possession in 1952.

AERIAL OF CONDOR FIELD. It is hard to believe, but the early builders of the Twentynine Palms airfield, named Condor Field, constructed it and the surrounding facilities right in the middle of the low-level drainage of a large salt flat. This photograph shows the aftermath of one of the heavy thunderstorms that rolls over the desert and the flooding that accompanies those storms. It also shows an extensive airfield complex that was used during World War II.

MAIN GATE, CONDOR FIELD. With the advent of World War II, a great many military airfields were constructed in Southern California. The fear of insurgents and saboteurs in California was great and airfields were ripe targets. Security at airfields appeared to be high, but in reality manpower shortages limited security to low levels. A few gate sentries and a roving patrol kept the tumbleweed off the runways. (Courtesy TPHS.)

GRADUATION CERTIFICATE. During the early days of World War II, everything was in short supply including aluminum, aircraft, and engines for aircraft. The obvious solution was a glider made of wood. Condor Field at Twentynine Palms, with its wide-open deserts, high winds, and rising thermals, was the perfect location for glider pilot training. The graduation certificate was awarded to a member of the 6th Army Air Force Glider Training Detachment Class 43-4-6. It was one of many awarded to departing students. (Courtesy TPHS.)

Class 43-4-6
6th AAFGTD

TWENTYNINE PALMS AIR ACADEMY

28 PALMS NAVAL AUXILIARY AIR STATION

TWENTYNINE PALMS. CALIFORNIA

TWENTYNINE PALMS NAVY AUXILIARY AIRFIELD. By 1944, the Army Air Corps' use of gliders had all but disappeared as more aircraft engines became available and more aircraft were being produced. The U.S. Navy took over Condor Field in 1944, calling it Twentynine Palms Naval Auxiliary Air Station. The navy used the Twentynine Palms air station for a variety of training purposes, flying a variety of aircraft in and out of Twentynine Palms. (Courtesy TPHS.)

11

F4F "WILDCAT" GRUMMAN FIGHTER. The 1930s saw a wealth of new aircraft designs and represented a significant period of aeronautical design advances and the eventual death of the biplane. However, many aircraft companies continued to develop excellent biplanes throughout the 1930s, and among those were the Grumman F3F-2 and Boeing F4B, both with airspeeds between 200 and 260 miles per hour. However, the Grumman F4F Wildcat monoplane increased airspeeds to 318 miles per hour, ending the era of biplanes. The development of the Wildcat began in 1936, and by 1941, the F4F-4 (the fourth model) arrived in service. The F4F-4 had folding wings for carrier operations, armor, and six machine guns instead of four. The added weight slowed the aircraft and shortened its range, but the armor made it much more durable in combat. (Courtesy FLAM.)

SNJ "TEXAN." The North American T-6 trainer, the Texan, had several names and was one of the all-time best aircraft designs. Over 17,000 Texans were constructed by plane builder North American and other companies licensed by North American. The Texan served in the air forces of at least 55 countries around the world. The airframe served many missions, including trainer, fighter, interceptor, forward air controller, fighter-bomber, and many others. (Courtesy FLAM.)

SBD DAUNTLESS, THE DOUGLAS DIVE-BOMBER. The SBD Dauntless is another early World War II aircraft that undoubtedly used the Twentynine Palms Navy Auxiliary Air Field. The SBD became famous throughout World War II fighting in nearly every major battle. Flying in high and then diving at a 70-degree dive angle, dropping a 500-pound bomb, was the SBD's hallmark. The plane was not exceptionally fast but had a gunner in the back seat with a dual .30-caliber machine gun for protection. (Courtesy FLAM.)

F4U CORSAIR VOUGHT. The F4U Corsair was known as "Whistling Death" by the Japanese during World War II. Initially constructed by the Vought Aircraft Company, 5,559 were eventually built. During the initial test trials, the Corsair flew a record 405 miles per hour. However, during the aircraft carrier test trials, the aircraft, or perhaps more accurately the pilots, had difficulty landing on aircraft carriers, relegating the Corsair to being a land-based fighter for a period. (Courtesy FLAM.)

SB2C "HELLDIVER" CURTISS. Another aircraft commonly frequenting the skies of naval airfields during the 1940s was the Helldiver. Not a popular aircraft among pilots, the aircraft earned a variety of other derogatory names over the course of its existence. The Helldiver was rushed through the testing and evaluation phase because the navy needed aircraft during the days leading up to World War II. During flight testing in a dive-bombing sequence, the aircraft's right wing and tail failed, sending the aircraft crashing to the ground. Not discouraged, the navy ordered 370. (Courtesy FLAM.)

F6F GRUMMAN "HELLCAT." The Grumman Hellcat and the Vought Corsair were the navy's and marines's top two fighters of World War II. The Hellcat started off as an upgraded F4F Wildcat but grew on the design table into a completely new fighter. With 5,163 victories over enemy aircraft, the Hellcat became the U.S. Navy's and Marine Corps' most successful fighter. Over 11,000 Hellcats were built in two years with a total production of 12,272. (Courtesy FLAM.)

Two

MARINES ARRIVE

The marines took over Twentynine Palms in 1952 when post–World War II and Korean War lessons learned dictated the need for heavier artillery units and guided-missile battalions. The existing facilities at Camp Lejeune, North Carolina, and Camp Pendleton, California, had limited space and ranges. Early Twentynine Palms tenants found sparse facilities and lived under adverse conditions while new construction occurred, and the marines in essence rebuilt the base.

In 1957, the base was designated as Marine Corps Base Twentynine Palms and the 1st Field Artillery Group (1st FAG), Force Troops, FMF Pacific became the primary tenant. The 1st FAG grew out of a reorganization effort by the Marine Corps dating to 1956 that changed the primary structure of marine artillery from battalions to batteries. Of the early units sent to Twentynine Palms, D Company 7th Engineer Battalion stands out because of the many construction projects it completed to enhance quality of life on the base for marines and their families. D Company also completed projects that facilitated military training; D Company 7th Engineer Battalion built everything from weapons ranges and buildings to a soccer field, a nine-hole golf course, and an 18-hole miniature golf course, which opened in 1964 with a fee of 15¢.

In 1966, the Marine Corps Communication-Electronics School Battalion (MCCES) began relocation to Twentynine Palms from Marine Corps Recruit Depot San Diego, initially with 500 marines. The MCCES eventually grew to include 2,500 more personnel. From its first days until the present, the Twentynine Palms military facility has changed and advanced with the times, adding new equipment and meeting the new challenges facing the defense of America. Twentynine Palms plays a vital role at a key locality in the maintenance of that defense.

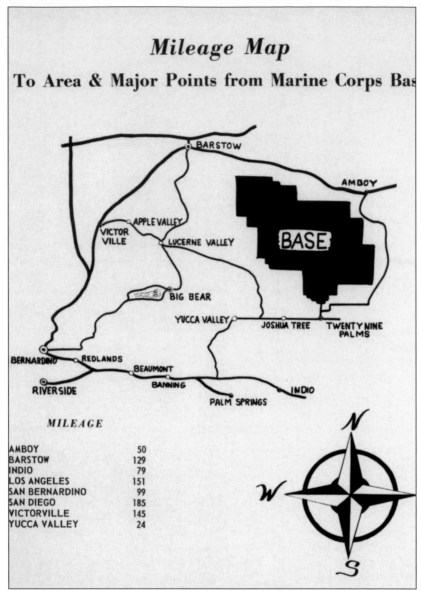

Mileage Map

To Area & Major Points from Marine Corps Base

BARSTOW
AMBOY
APPLE VALLEY
VICTOR VILLE
LUCERNE VALLEY
BASE
BIG BEAR
YUCCA VALLEY
JOSHUA TREE
TWENTYNINE PALMS
BERNARDINO
REDLANDS
BEAUMONT
RIVERSIDE
BANNING
INDIO
PALM SPRINGS

MILEAGE

AMBOY	50
BARSTOW	129
INDIO	79
LOS ANGELES	151
SAN BERNARDINO	99
SAN DIEGO	185
VICTORVILLE	145
YUCCA VALLEY	24

MILEAGE MAP. This mileage map provides a good glimpse of how isolated Twentynine Palms is from civilization. In the early days of World War II, travel to and from the community was an undertaking of significant proportions. Even on today's modern highways, it takes a few hours to reach popular destinations like Las Vegas, the Colorado River, Laughlan, and Palm Springs. Nearby Joshua Tree National Park is a natural and geological wonderland. At a nearly perfect altitude between 2,700 and 3,500 feet, it is usually 10 degrees cooler than the low desert in the summertime and 20 degrees warmer than the mountains in the wintertime. Yucca Valley, at 3,300 feet, also provides moderate high-desert temperatures, clean air, and incredible clear star-filled nights and has been recommended by many doctors for people suffering with respiratory problems. Dating to the 1880s, Yucca Valley's history was built around cattle and mining. However, the mines ran out and the last cattle drive went through town in 1947. Palm Springs, less than an hour from Twentynine Palms, has adapted to become a golfer's paradise and ground zero for resort living in southern California.

MARINES ARRIVE. In grand style, the Marine Corps arrives in Twentynine Palms in 1952, marching down Highway 62 to the cheers of many local onlookers. As few as 120 marines arrived as part of an advance party to begin upgrading the abandoned buildings and infrastructure remaining from World War II. Over the next couple years, this contingent of marines lived in old, run-down buildings with few amenities while they initiated rebuilding a base abandoned since World War II.

BY AIR, LAND, OR SEA. The C-119 "Flying Boxcar" was used to bring troops and supplies into Marine Corps Base Twentynine Palms throughout the 1950s. (Courtesy FLAM.)

C-119 FLYING BOXCAR. During the 1950s and the early days of construction and expansion at Twentynine Palms, delivering supplies and personnel by air was a regular occurrence because of the remoteness of the base. These C-119s landed at the old Condor Field runways. The clamshell doors on the C-119 allowed for the disembarkation of small vehicles and cargo. Side doors were used for para-operations. Pilots and crews also knew the C-119 as the "Whistling Outhouse." (Courtesy FLAM.)

OLD HOSPITAL. The old Twentynine Palms hospital provided the base with a first-class medical treatment center for marines and their dependents. It was situated between two helicopter landing zones to facilitate transporting injured marines from anywhere on the enormous military reservation to the hospital in minutes.

MESS HALL, 1964. Standing in line at the mess hall in the 1960s was simply a fact of life in the "old corps," as was standing in line for just about everything else. This mess hall was used primarily by marines from Force Troops. It was the classic mess hall with the silver metal trays and large portions of "mystery meat" on the menu with "hard-corps" mess chefs yelling, "Hurry up!" as soldiers sidestepped down the chow line. Modern Marine Corps mess halls are more akin to restaurant buffets. (Courtesy Oliver Wiley.)

FAMILY ACTIVITIES. Twentynine Palms is a remote, isolated location, but there are many activities, functions, recreational sites, and facilities on or near the base for marines and their families. In addition to swimming pools, Twentynine Palms has a very nice and surprisingly, considering the average temperature, green golf course. This is a 1960s photograph of a group enjoying 45-revolution-per-minute records at one of the family activities.

PING-PONG. Ping-Pong at the youth center has always been a lot of fun. Marine bases at remote locations like Twentynine Palms are often the most enjoyable duty stations because extra efforts are taken to provide activities for marines and their families.

TOWED HOWITZER. Twentynine Palms outdoor static displays running along the main road through the military installation include a variety of historic military weapons and one aircraft. Viewing these static displays, one can get a feeling for the steady evolution of artillery, tanks, and amphibians over the years. The 105-mm M101A1 towed howitzer has a crew of eight and first appeared in service during World War II. Versions of the 105-mm howitzer have been mounted on aircraft as early as World War II, during Vietnam, and currently on the Hercules AC-130.

SELF-PROPELLED HOWITZER. The M-53 155-mm howitzer weighs 49 tons. It has a crew of six and carries 10 projectiles. The vehicle carries enough fuel to travel 160 miles. The gun shoots a projectile up to 10.5 miles. The M-53 saw service from 1956 to 1969.

AMPHIBIOUS ASSAULT VEHICLE. The Landing Vehicle Track (howitzer)-6, known as the LVTH-6, served as the amphibious artillery piece of its day. It could land on a beachhead and move inland, providing artillery support to commanders in the field long before towed artillery pieces arrived on the beach. The LVTH-6 weighed 13 tons, carried 100 rounds of 105-mm artillery, and had a range of 7 miles. The vehicle has a crew of six and saw service between 1954 and 1969.

HEAVY ARTILLERY. The M110A2 eight-inch self-propelled howitzer weighed 26 tons. It carried 30 projectiles that had a range of 14.5 miles and a crew of 12. The vehicle had a speed up to 40 miles per hour. It saw service from 1963 until the early 1990s.

SELF-PROPELLED ONTOS. The M-50 ONTOS weighed nine and a half tons and carried a crew of three and 18 projectiles. It could travel 150 miles on one tank of gas. The six 106-mm recoilless rifles it carried had a range of 1,100 meters. The ONTOS saw service from 1955 to 1970.

24

MAIN BATTLE TANK. The M60A1 tank weighed 53.5 tons and had a crew of four. Its range with a full load of fuel was 240 miles at cruising speeds. The M60A1 armament was a 105-mm gun that had a range of 3,000 meters, and it also carried a 7.62-mm machine gun and a .50-caliber machine gun. The M60A1 saw service between 1975 and 1991.

SKYHAWK AT TWENTYNINE PALMS. This A4 Skyhawk is included in the static displays to recognize that a large part of the activity at Twentynine Palms is aviation related. The squadron represented on the A4's fuselage, "The Avengers," dates to the early days of World War II when VMF211 landed on Wake Island and participated in the famous marine defense against overwhelming Japanese forces.

CURRENT SWIMMING FACILITY. The swimming facility at Twentynine Palms is one of the nicest on any military facility, accommodating marines and their families most of the year. During unbearable summer days, the swimming facility is undoubtedly the favorite place on the base.

NON-COMS GATHERING SPOT. The Staff Non-Commissioned Officers Club has always been one of the best-attended facilities on any Marine Corps base. SNCOs discuss the hot issues of the day, the commandant's book list, their military education courses, and undoubtedly exchange "kind" remarks about the new lieutenant who just reported for duty.

"THE ZONE." During off-duty hours, The Zone provides video games, pool tables, internet access, and a movie room for marines to zone out and relieve some stress after a hard day of combat training. Quality of life issues are a large part of the Marine Corps overall plan to make days better for its marines who are always far from home.

FOOD COURT. The Twentynine Palms military base has a variety of commercial food outlets for marines and their families to enjoy. Taco Bell, Subway, and a popular pizza place are among a few of the options. Since physical fitness and military appearance is a stalwart fundamental of the Marine Corps culture, some marines are calling for a Souplantation and a sushi bar.

STATION THEATER. The Combat Center Auditorium was built soon after the marines arrived at Twentynine Palms in the early 1950s but has been remodeled since to a modern facility that shows all the big-screen hits. Movies at marine bases were free in the past, but inflation gradually caught up, and in the 1960s, the Marine Corps started charging 10¢ for a movie. Riots almost ensued, because at the time, 10¢ was a lot of money. Today movies are free on many marine bases.

MARINE CORPS EXCHANGE. The Marine Corps Exchange is basically an upscale Marine Corps Wal-Mart. In addition to having all the necessities of Marine Corps life, the Exchange usually stocks many top-of-the-line retail items and is a favorite hangout for marines during their off-duty hours.

MODERN BARRACKS. These are being built on every Marine Corps base, and Twentynine Palms is no exception. Living accommodations for the Marine Corps today much closer resembles life in a college dormitory than the "old corps" squad bays with group showers and the not very popular "on-line" toilets, not to mention the involuntary "steam cleanings" everyone enjoyed every time the commode was flushed without warning everyone in the shower.

OFFICER'S CLUB. The Officer's Club is the center of social activity for all warrant and commissioned officers. It is one of several clubs built for marines generally broken down by rank. Camaraderie in the Marine Corps is almost as strong in the clubs as it is in the foxhole. Many careers have been made and lost in the clubs that often serve as testing grounds. The Officer's Club also has a dining room that almost always can be counted on to have a "Mongolian beef" night.

OFFICER'S CLUB SWIMMING POOL. The Officer's Club swimming pool at Twentynine Palms is much smaller than the main swimming pool, but on a hot summer day it serves its purpose well. Families and dependents of officers stationed at Twentynine Palms find the pool its own oasis during those torrid days.

LAKE BANDINI. The sewage treatment plant is referred to by many as Lake Bandini, which is a reference to an old fertilizer commercial. It is also referred to by some as the officer's swimming facility. There is a rumor that when jet pilots visit the base and spend too much time at the Officer's Club, they have races swimming across the length of Lake Bandini after the club closes.

TWENTYNINE PALMS HEADQUARTERS BUILDING. The commanding general, or the "CG," of the base presides over the many functions, operations, services, and security of the base, to mention a few duties. The CG is located in the Headquarters Building, which is adjacent to the parade deck. The CG's flag flies on a flagpole in front of the building displaying the number of stars he wears on his collar. When the CG is out of town, the flag is taken down.

PARADE DECK. The parade deck, seen here and on the next page, is a multifunctional facility allowing the base command to have large military parades and ceremonies such as change of commands and retirement ceremonies. Practicing marching and the manual of arms are also favorite Marine Corps training exercises.

PARADE DECK. This parade deck also serves as an emergency landing zone for helicopters delivering medical evacuees from the field to the base hospital.

CATHOLIC CHAPEL. Military chapels are generally multi-faith, but during the early construction at Twentynine Palms, the marines built a Catholic chapel, seen here and on the opposite page, on one side of the parade deck and a Protestant chapel on the other. In both views, the Catholic chapel is decorated for Christmas.

CHAPEL. Chapels are among the most popular places on any base where marines find comfort from enormous physical and mental stresses of everyday training, expectations, and demands placed upon them.

ANOTHER CHAPEL VIEW. In addition to many social activities, chapels accommodate weddings, baptisms, promotions, and almost any social function imaginable—a hub of the military community.

NON-COM CAMARADERIE. The Non-Commissioned Officers Club is a place for marines of the rank of corporal and sergeant. It provides many of the amenities of a social club for generally younger marines to gather and socialize. It also provides a forum for junior NCOs to interact and mature in an environment of their own that is not subject to the total scrutiny from senior NCOs and officers they face almost everywhere else on the base.

EAST GYM AND FITNESS CENTER. Physical fitness is another of the fundamentals of Marine Corps life and culture. Every marine base has at least one state-of-the-art physical fitness center filled with a variety of ways to torture oneself and endure a variety of excruciating exercises in the name of physical health. No military service in the world can boast of having members in better shape than the Marine Corps.

THE "O COURSE." The Marine Corps obstacle course, seen here and on the next page, tests an individual's upper-body strength, agility, and endurance. This training facility is known by the nickname "O Course."

SEPARATING THE MEN FROM THE BOYS. In some Marine Corps schools, where physical fitness is even more common than everywhere else, marines run the O Course four times consecutively and are timed. This separates the men from the boys. The 20-foot rope at the end of the course is the real challenge, but many marines climb the rope using no feet.

RAPPELLING PLATFORM. At the top of the rappelling platform, an old UH-1 "Huey" helicopter fuselage sits to aid marines in their training. Using a combination of ropes and braking rings, rappelling is fairly easy once a person gets the feel for braking. Marines also "fast rope" from the back of helicopters, which is little more than sliding down a rope wearing gloves, much like a fireman slides down a pole in the firehouse.

Three

MARINE TRAINING AT TWENTYNINE PALMS

After taking possession of the Twentynine Palms military reservation in 1952, the marines spent the next decade in a massive effort to upgrade the base infrastructure. This included improvements to everything from ordnance ranges to bowling alleys. The obvious purpose of Twentynine Palms was the training of marines and the testing and development of equipment. Since 1952, the ranges have been continually upgraded to include electronic moving targets and accommodate modern weaponry. The quality of life function of the base has also continued to improve with new facilities and nearly continuous upgrades.

Shortly after being established at Twentynine Palms in the mid-1950s, the 1st Field Artillery Group reorganized Force Artillery at Twentynine Palms, launching intense artillery exercises, testing new equipment, and training personnel. In essence, these exercises took the Marine Corps to the next level of preparedness. During the 1950s and 1960s, cold war–threat missile technology became an important weapon in the arsenal, and the Marine Corps added the Honest John and Terrier missiles to the inventory. They were followed by the Hawk missile system. As missile technology progressed, the portable missile evolved in the form of the Red Eye and Stinger, followed by Dragon, Javelin, and TOW systems among others.

Twentynine Palms has played a fundamental role in the development and deployment of these systems and the training of marines to effectively use them in combat. One of the newest units and technologies to be found at Twentynine Palms is the Unmanned Aerial Vehicles Squadron, which is a premium example of how the facility is essential in keeping the Marine Corps modern.

ARTILLERY IN WARFARE. The first self-propelled artillery weapons appeared as early as World War I, but by World War II, most artillery pieces were still being towed by horses or mules and eventually by vehicles. The Korean War provided a few advancements, but the post–Korean War years marked significant progress in self-propelled artillery technology. Better tracks and engines provided greater reliability and mobility, while rocket-propelled shells added significantly to the weapon's range. Two of the primary weapons of the 1st Field Artillery Group in the 1950s and 1960s were the 155-mm and 8-inch, self-propelled howitzers.

SELF-PROPELLED HOWITZER. The M-55 self-propelled howitzer was developed in 1958 and used until the early 1970s. Although it did not have much in the way of armor or protection for its crew, it was a popular weapon by virtue of its capability. With a little more than 2 inches in diameter over a 155-mm howitzer, the 8-inch delivered a wallop upon enemy positions. In 1957, the 1st FAG consisted of 155-mm self-propelled gun batteries; 8-inch, self-propelled howitzer batteries; Honest John rocket battery (Honest John); and a headquarters battery. Here 8-inch, self-propelled howitzers prepare for a firing exercise.

HONEST JOHN ROCKET. The Honest John is a long-range artillery rocket capable of carrying an atomic or high-explosive warhead. It is a free-flight rocket as opposed to a guided missile. The rocket was 27 feet long, 30 inches in diameter, and weighed 5,800 pounds with a range of 12 miles. First deployed in 1954, it was the first U.S. tactical nuclear weapon. In 1961, an improved version was produced that increased its range.

TERRIER MISSILES. In June 1956, the 1st Medium Antiaircraft Missile Battalion arrived at Twentynine Palms with the Terrier guided missile as its primary weapon. The Terrier is a medium-range, all-weather, surface-to-air missile designed to extend the range of conventional antiaircraft weapons. Missile/rocket technology and development became a high priority during World War II, when the Germans began launching V rockets toward cities in England. The United States spent the remainder of the 1940s and early 1950s trying to catch up to or duplicate the technology the Germans possessed in the early 1940s.

HAWK MISSILES. The 1st and 2nd Light Antiaircraft Missile Battalions arrived at Twentynine Palms in the early 1960s with the Hawk missile system. The Hawk is an extremely mobile guided-missile system that can engage extremely low-flying targets and maintain a high rate of fire.

BASIC RIFLEMAN. The Marine Corps is the only branch of the military service in the entire world that can boast of having every member qualified and competent with their assigned weapon. Every marine, according to the commandant, is a basic rifleman. Every marine goes to the rifle range in boot camp and initially qualifies with, currently, the M-16 rifle. Every few years thereafter, each marine returns to the range to requalify with his or her primary weapon. (Courtesy U.S. Navy.)

DEFENDING AGAINST AIR ATTACK. The Hawk missile system was designed to provide defense against air attack. Placed into service in 1962, the Hawk missile weighs 300 pounds, using a solid-propellant fuel with a rocket-motorized missile, and has a range of 23 miles to a ceiling of 30,000 feet. The system can fire one missile every three seconds.

SNIPER'S VIEW. The sniper has been a critical battlefield asset since the early days of combat rifles. Early rifles did not have long ranges, limiting a sniper's effectiveness. However, as rifled barrels were invented and better ammunition became available, the opportunities grew. As early as the American Revolution, American snipers became infamous in British circles for shooting officers at very long ranges. The M82A1A .50-caliber rifle, currently in use, is effective to 1,800 meters. (Courtesy U.S. Navy.)

RIFLE RANGE. The Marine Corps at Twentynine Palms has a plethora of ranges for every weapon imaginable, from rifles and pistols to guided missiles and rockets. There are even ranges for artillery and jets and helicopters. Here marines are practicing firing in the sitting position.

CONTROL ON THE RANGE. The range officer in the control tower barks commands over the loudspeaker to ensure everyone knows when and when not to fire; range accidents are rare as a result of their total command of the firing line. Marksmanship instructors kneel alongside a marine offering advice and tips to help improve his shooting score, a part of each marine's qualifications for promotion.

COMBAT TOWN. Combat Town is a stage designed to allow marines to train for fighting in an urban setting. Door-to-door battles are some of the most difficult and dangerous types of combat, and they require teamwork and communication with the entire unit. (Courtesy U.S. Navy.)

GAS-MASK ORIENTEERING. Modern chemical warfare and the use of poisonous fumes began during World War I, when the Germans first used chlorine gas to attack French positions in 1915. The British built a carbon monoxide gas mask, or respirator, a few months prior to the first German attack, when they discovered that unexploded enemy artillery shells gave off levels of carbon monoxide high enough to kill soldiers in trenches and foxholes. About the same time, a Canadian designed a mask with chemical filters that neutralized the chlorine used by the Germans. These masks were eventually used by the Allies and are considered to be the first masks used to protect against chemical weapons. In 1916, the larger filter drums were added to masks by the Germans and British, providing better protection against deadly chemicals. The most reliable mask used during World War I was the British Small Box Respirator (SBR).

GAS-MASK TRAINING. Marines learn to put their gas masks on, clear them, and breathe normally in less than 11 seconds. They practice this skill inside a gas chamber, where they are then told to take the mask off and recite a couple verses of the Marine Corps Hymn. Knowing what the gas smells and tastes like, and what it does to the eyes, nose, and skin, gives one a better appreciation for the gas mask. Field exercises wearing a gas mask are extremely demanding and difficult. Standing idle wearing a gas mask is one thing, but walking, hiking, and running wearing a gas mask is a total test of one's physical conditioning and endurance. (Courtesy U.S. Navy.)

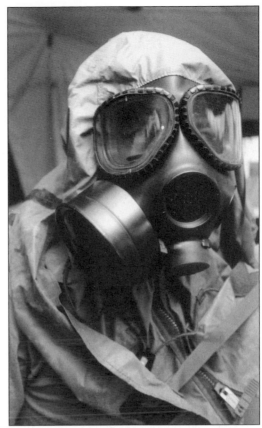

MACHINE-GUN TRAINING. The M-60 was type classified by the army in 1957 and has had a long and distinguished career. It fires a NATO 7.62-mm (.308 inches) round and is used as a general crew-served weapon. It has a removable barrel to prevent overheating and can be fired from a tripod or a bipod and is also mounted on helicopters. The M60E3 is the newer, lightweight version of the M-60. The reduction in weight has meant a loss of reliability, and troop acceptance of the M-60E3 is poor.

RANGE TOWER. Range towers can be found all over Twentynine Palms. They provide a clear view of not only the firing line but what is going on downrange. It is not uncommon for a stray helicopter to fly over a live firing range or a lost PFC driving a HMMWV (high-mobility, multipurpose wheeled vehicle) looking for the MCX. Fires are a common side effect of live firing ranges. Dry desert brush and tumbleweeds can turn a pleasant day into a disaster if they ignite on a windy day.

"FIRE AND FORGET." The Javelin is a portable and disposable "fire and forget" antitank and antiarmored vehicle missile that is intended to replace the Dragon missile system. The Javelin has a range of 2,500 meters and has secondary capabilities against helicopters and ground emplacements. The Javelin has dual-warhead capability, making it much more lethal than the Dragon missile.

REDEYE MISSILES. The Redeye is a portable air-defense system that first entered the inventory in the 1960s. It was intended to provide combat units with a defensive weapon against low-flying enemy aircraft, helicopters, or drones. The missile is a rocket-propelled, heat-seeking missile that can be detonated in three ways: by penetrating the target, by an inertia-sensing device, or by a self-destruct system. In 1958, Redeye human factors tests were conducted at Twentynine Palms to determine its feasibility in combat. It is a supersonic missile with an infrared sensor in the nose, which resulted in the name "Redeye." The missile was used for more than two decades and was replaced by the Stinger. In 1961, a marine officer test fired the Redeye for the first time to evaluate noise, recoil, heat, and other possible negative effects to the user. None were noted, but other problems occurred and deployment of the missile was delayed pending modifications. By 1968, the first Redeyes were deployed by the army. Throughout its life, it was constantly upgraded and refined, but by the early 1990s, the system was terminated.

MORTARS AT TWENTYNINE PALMS. Mortars were developed early in the transition from catapults to artillery, probably based on the need to lob artillery rounds over castle walls while canons drilled holes in the walls with direct fire. Mortars are also effective against dug-in troops and targets in defilade. The U.S. military uses 60-mm light mortars, 81-mm medium mortars, and the 107-mm and 120-mm heavy mortars. Mortars allow battlefield commanders to place killing fire on a nearby enemy quickly and independently of supporting artillery.

SWIFT VEHICLES AND THEIR WEAPONRY. The M151 series Jeep, and later the HMMWV, provided a versatile weapons platform for many weapon combinations. Here a TOW missile system is mounted on the Jeep.

VEHICLES AND WEAPONRY. A TOW missile system is mounted to the HMMWV in this image, but the possibilities are endless. Among the many weapons affixed to highly mobile vehicles are Gattling guns, .50-caliber machine guns, the MK19 grenade launcher, and many others.

JEEP WITH GATTLING GUN. Long before Hannibal placed the first heavy archers upon elephants, weapons mobility has been a key factor in the outcome of any conflict. The marines have long experimented with vehicle-mounted weapons, and this Jeep/Gattling gun combination is just one example.

JEEP WITH GATTLING GUN. Here is another Jeep/Gattling gun combination. The M151 Jeep, although famous in its own right, did not have the durability, speed, or mobility to withstand the military challenges of the late 20th and early 21st centuries. The M151's tendency to flip was exacerbated by placing a top-heavy weapon system upon it. The M151 also used highly flammable unleaded fuel, increasing the risk of ignition during a firefight. Current fast-attack vehicles use diesel fuel.

HOWITZER FIREPOWER. This is a 105-mm towed howitzer. The advent of artillery began with the discovery of gunpowder in approximately 850 AD in China. Firecrackers became hand grenades and were used militarily by the Chinese in 919 AD, evolving into "flinging" larger bombs by catapult, which evolved into rocketry. Records are sketchy, but one of the first rockets was fired using a bamboo tube during a battle in 1132 AD. The Arabs improved gunpowder and used cannons against the Spanish in 1325 AD. By the early 1300s, the use of artillery had spread across Europe.

FIELD ARTILLERY PIECE. The 105-mm howitzer is a light, towed, general-purpose field artillery weapon. It can be used for direct or indirect fire. It is single loaded and air cooled using semi-fixed ammunition. The recoil mechanism is a constant hydro-pneumatic type that decreases the energy of the recoil, gradually avoiding violent movement of the weapon upon discharge.

THE 155-MM HOWITZER. Although marines served as artillerymen with General Washington's army in 1777, the corps was primarily an infantry organization until the early 1850s. In 1853, Archibald Henderson, the commandant of the Marine Corps, recommended that certain units should be equipped with artillery, which at that time meant a 3-inch field gun. In 1857, the commandant sent 1st Lt. Israel Green to West Point to receive artillery training. In 1959, a navy order stated that marines would be employed as gun crews aboard ships. Marine artillery grew slowly prior to World War I during the Spanish-American War, deployments to China, Vera Cruz, Mexico, and the Dominican Republic. The first full marine artillery regiment was formed in 1918 as the 11th Marine Regiment and was quickly redesignated the 10th Artillery Regiment. During World War II, the need for marine artillery expanded exponentially, and the first 155-mm howitzer battalions were formed.

UPGRADING HOWITZERS. The M-109 155-mm self-propelled howitzer was introduced in the early 1960s and has been continually upgraded to today's version, the M109A6. The crew of the early M109 consists of a section chief, driver, gunner, three cannoneers who load and fire the weapon, and two gunners who handle the ammunition. The M109A6 Paladin needs only one cannoneer and two ammunition handlers for a total crew of six.

POWERFUL HOWITZER. The M-198 medium-towed howitzer is a 155-mm field artillery weapon. It is transportable by the CH-53E Super Stallion helicopter or C-130 fixed-wing transport aircraft. The M-198 provides increased range, reliability, and maintainability over the previous model. The use of rocket-assisted projectiles significantly extends the range and lethality of the weapon. The first M198 howitzers were delivered to the 10th Marine Regiment in January 1982.

TANK TERRITORY. Twentynine Palms may be the perfect training facility for tracked vehicles. Hundreds of square miles of open terrain, dry lake beds, mountains, and rocky lava beds provide the terrain, the climate, and the challenges marines will face in similar combat theaters. The U.S. military did not always have the best tanks on the battlefield. However, during Desert Storm, the M1A1 battle tank proved itself to be the premier tank in the world.

MARINE TANK HISTORY. The Marine Corps established the light tank platoon in 1923 at Quantico, Virginia, equipping it with a six-ton, French 1917 Renault tank that mounted a .30-caliber machine gun. The unit was deployed to China in 1927, where it conducted operations for 18 months. In the 1930s, the marines experimented with the Marmon-Harrington five-ton tank with a .50-caliber machine gun. Although it was more adaptable for amphibious operations, it was not reliable.

MARINE TANKS IN THE SOLOMON ISLANDS. During World War II, the marines had tanks at Guadalcanal but really first used them in battle at Bougainville using the M4A2 Sherman. Flamethrower tanks were used extensively at Saipan and Iwo Jima and later on Okinawa. By the Korean War, the corps was using the M26 Pershing and eventually fielded the M46 as its primary tank between 1951 and 1953. In 1958, the M48A1 tank entered the corps' arsenal, followed by the M103 Heavy Tank and the M67, a flamethrower variant of the M48. All these tanks saw duty in Vietnam.

ABRAMS TANK IN DESERT STORM. The M-60 tank was next used by the corps in 1975. This was followed by the development of the M1 Abrams in the early 1980s, which was upgraded to the M1A1 and M1A2. The newer model Abrams tanks have a 120-mm M256 smoothbore gun that fires a variety of rounds. The tank commander has a 12.7-mm M2 machine gun, and the loader has a 7.62-mm machine gun. Another M240 machine gun is mounted on the right side of the tank. The Marine Corps use of the Abrams during Desert Storm was of historical magnitude.

GETTING MARINES ASHORE. The Amphibious Assault Vehicle (AAV), also known as the AMTRAC by seasoned marines, is an armored, full-tracked, landing vehicle with a primary mission of transporting troops from ship to shore. The AAV can also travel inland upon reaching land and cruises at 25 miles per hour on land, 6 miles per hour in the water, and has a range of 100 miles. The AAV can carry 21 fully combat–equipped marines.

TO THE SHORES OF TRIPOLI. Here is another AAV. Landing armed troops on foreign soil undoubtedly predates even the ancient Greek and Persian military campaigns. The Romans advanced the concept significantly as did the Vikings and later the Spanish and English. The U.S. Marines, although serving off naval ships since 1775 and performing ship-to-shore duties in places like Tripoli, began to perfect modern amphibious assaults in the 1920s and 1930s in anticipation of a war with Japan in the Pacific. (Courtesy U.S. Navy.)

AMTRACS IN WORLD WAR II. It became obvious during the preplanning for World War II that a motorized amphibious vehicle was required to transport men, equipment, and supplies from naval vessels around and over jagged reefs and unfriendly beaches into battle in the Pacific. In 1940, the marines chose the Landing Vehicle Track (LVT-1), commonly called the AMTRAC for amphibious tractor. Over the next three years, 1,125 LVTs were built mostly by the Food Machinery Corporation. (Courtesy U.S. Navy.)

TOUGH LESSONS OF TARAWA. The LVT-1 performed notably during World War II, but it needed help. The suspension and paddle treads on its tracks were easily damaged on rough terrain, and it was slow on land and sea, making it an easy target. Its lack of armor made it easy prey for beachhead defensive guns. Even with improvised armor during the battle of Tarawa, 75 percent of the LVT's used were lost in three days of fighting in November 1943. Modern AAV's have corrected these flaws, providing the Marine Corps with an outstanding fighting vehicle. (Courtesy U.S. Navy.)

LIGHT ARMORED VEHICLE (LAV). During the 1970s, the Department of Defense recognized a requirement for a rapid-deployment force. The Marine Corps began testing the LAV in 1980 at Twentynine Palms. In 1982, the Marine Corps contracted for LAV production, and in May 1985, the corps began receiving its first LAVs. It is an extremely versatile and strategically mobile vehicle designed to engage the enemy anywhere in the battle area. It has a range of 410 miles, a ground speed up to 60 miles per hour, and a swim speed of 6 miles per hour. It is an all-terrain, all-weather vehicle equipped with night-vision capabilities.

USES OF THE LAV. The LAV can be configured for a variety of missions: reconnaissance, command and control, logistics, recovery, antitank, air defense, or mortar. The mortar configuration provides indirect fire support for infantry and reconnaissance forces as well as smoke and illumination.

SUPPLIES ABOARD AN LAV. The logistics LAV configuration equips the vehicle to supply everything from petroleum, oil, and lubricants to ammunition and food rations. All the configurations are equipped with a weapons package, including the M240E1 machine gun, the M252 81-mm mortar, the M901 TOW II antitank guided missile, and the M242 25-mm chain gun.

LAV ADAPTABILITY. The command-and-control LAV is an all-weather, all-terrain vehicle with night capabilities and is transportable via the C-130 Hercules transport aircraft or CH53E Super Stallion helicopter. This version LAV can carry 1,000 rounds of 7.62-mm ammunition and a variety of smoke grenades and other ordnance. The vehicle can be made fully amphibious within three minutes.

Four

EXPEDITIONARY AIR FIELD AND AVIATION

The concept of an expeditionary airfield began either as a result of necessity or mechanical failure shortly after the first aviators took to the skies. As the military expanded its use of the aircraft and eventually the helicopter, a frequent occurrence was that someone on the ground needed something from someone in the air or vice versa. Usually these happenstances seemed to never occur near an airport. Landing in farmers' fields to rescue downed pilots, to perform medical extractions, or to exchange communiqués with ground forces was a common occurrence as early as World War I.

Marines took the concept to the next level almost immediately after that conflict ended. In 1919, marines deployed to Haiti and throughout the Caribbean islands, where they would stay throughout the 1920s and 1930s, in addition to Guam and China. Landing on mountain airstrips and on swaths cut into the jungle scarcely wider than the aircraft's landing gear or wing tips became a well-practiced art form. In World War II, the Marine Corps found itself on an island-hopping campaign in the Pacific Ocean, building new airfields or conquering Japanese airstrips along the way. However, the excessive rains and sandy soils in the south Pacific hampered runway operations. Born of necessity, the expeditionary airfield (EAF) evolved.

The industrious and often ingenious marines, combined with American industrial creativity, began developing runway materials, portable matting, lighting, portable control towers, communications equipment, navigation aids, and portable refueling stations. These were followed by all-terrain crash-crew vehicles and eventually arresting gear until, by the 1960s, the Marine Corps could setup an expeditionary airfield almost anywhere in a very short time. In 1976, the marines built a training EAF at Twentynine Palms to provide air and ground training to its forces.

EARLY AVIATION OPERATIONS. When the Marine Corps took possession of Twentynine Palms in 1952, the old airfield, called Condor Field, remained. Although dilapidated after years of neglect, the runways were functional and air operations and training were conducted prior to building the EAF 10 miles west of Condor Field. The helicopters of the 1950s and 1960s certainly took advantage of the extensive training opportunities at Twentynine Palms, as well as fixed-wing aircraft able to use the facilities. Here the corps' "helo" workhorse from the Korean War, the H-19 Chickasaw, disembarks troops during a field exercise.

KOREAN WAR HELICOPTER. The H-19 Chickasaw entered service in the Marine Corps during the Korean War in the early 1950s, when the corps was pioneering helicopter-assault tactics and strategies as well as rapid helicopter medical evacuations of combat-wounded marines from the battlefield. The H-19's first flight was on November 10, 1949, and it entered operations in 1950. Over 1,100 H-19s were manufactured. The H-19 was christened under fire during the Korean War, where the Marine Corps pioneered its many uses, ranging from assault support, medical evacuations, combat resupply, and reconnaissance.

ANOTHER H-19 CHICKASAW. As commonplace as helicopter assaults are to the battlefield today, in the 1950s, they compared to the time Hannibal added elephants to his battlefield inventory. The H-19 performed in an outstanding manner during the Korean War, but it became immediately obvious that a more powerful and higher-performing helicopter was needed. The H-19's maximum weight was 8,070 pounds compared to the Sikorsky CH-53D Sea Stallion with a maximum gross weight of 42,000 pounds. The H-19s maximum forward air space was 90 knots versus 170 knots for the CH-53D. The H-19 was a pioneer for helicopter development and tactics.

MARINES DURING "PARA-OPS." Marines board a transport for paratroop duty or para-ops. Many marines earn their "jump wings," but they must continue practicing their trade thereafter to remain current and proficient. Typically, a jump sequence occurs about 1,200 feet above ground level into a field after winds are determined and offsets are established. However, some units also practice jumping into lakes or the ocean, which adds a significant degree of difficulty to surviving the landing. A marine reserve unit at Reno/Stead Airport in Nevada experimented with special oxygen equipment that permitted pilots flying RH-53D helicopters from Alameda, California, to climb to 16,500 feet, allowing a greater free fall for those parachuting out of the helicopters.

A "PARA-MARINE" LANDING. There appear to be many dangers associated with para-ops, but accidents are rare because the professionalism of the practitioners is high. Para-ops at Twentynine Palms can be dangerous, because the winds are often high and usually erratic.

SEA HORSE MEDEVAC. The CH-34 Sea Horse represented the next step in the evolution of Marine Corps helicopters after the H-19 Chickasaw. The CH-34 had a little more power but could not lift the heavy loads the Marine Corps needed to transport. The CH-34 performed brilliantly in the early days of the Vietnam War during Operation ShuFly, earning numerous Navy Cross awards for its aircrew. Here the HMM-163 "Evil Eyes" performs a medical evacuation during an exercise.

MOJAVE HEAVY-LIFTER. The CH-37 Mojave helicopter, shown as troops disembark, was delivered to the Marine Corps in the late 1950s and represented the corps' first heavy-lift helicopter. It had twin engines and five main rotor blades and was the first helicopter to have retractable land gear. The CH-37 had front-loading doors that opened to carry troops, vehicles, and/or cargo. The CH-37 was delivered in 1956 and could carry 26 fully equipped troops. Maximum takeoff weight for the CH-37 was 21,000 pounds while maximum forward airspeed was 114 knots. The windows in the front clamshell door presented a problem occasionally when the helicopter had bird strikes. The passengers in the cabin were showered with broken glass and bird parts.

MORE MOJAVE MUSCLE. The CH-37 was developed just prior to the development of turbine engines and had two heavier and less-powerful piston engines that limited its performance. It's seen here during external lift operations.

INTRUDER OVER EAF. During the 1950s and 1960s, the Marine Corps acquired several new jet aircraft including the A4 Skyhawk, F4 Phantom II, and the A6 Intruder. These aircraft were used a great amount during the Vietnam War and all used the Twentynine Palms ranges extensively prior to the construction of the Twentynine Palms Expeditionary Air Field. Here an A6 Intruder flies over the EAF runways in preparation for landing.

COBRAS ON EAF RAMP. The EAF ramp can accommodate many squadrons of helicopters and jets, but hangar space is extremely limited. Most of the aircraft servicing and work is done outdoors, when aircraft surface temperatures can approach 150 degrees Fahrenheit. Mechanics have to hide their tools in the shade or else they become too hot to pick up. On cold and windy days, working outdoors on top of an aircraft can be very dangerous, but learning these lessons prior to going to war is the entire purpose.

FLAG OVER TENT CAMP AT CAMP WILSON. Camp Wilson is the name of the camp adjacent to the EAF. In years past, as many as 5,000 marines might descend on Camp Wilson for Combined Arms Exercises (CAXs) and deploy to the surrounding areas for combat training. Until recently, the standard combat tent or the aluminum siding A-frame was used for billeting. The A-frames were much cooler than the tents and held up much better on windy days.

HOME AWAY FROM HOME. Living in a canvas tent in the desert had two obvious advantages over not having a tent: shade and protection from the high winds. However, the dirt floor did little to protect occupants from ants, scorpions, lizards, and snakes. During the day, the side flaps would roll up to hopefully catch a breeze in the 100-plus degree heat, but when the breeze turned into a blow, everyone's sleeping bags and gear would be covered in inches of sand and dirt.

ALL-IMPORTANT CAMARADERIE. It is no understatement that CAXs offer unlimited opportunities to get to know the other members of your unit—intimately. After a very short time, isolation in remote areas reveals a marine's inner person, which can take a variety of unique forms. Occasionally, some marines just run off into the desert, but most work extremely hard on duty and can be found supporting each other off duty. Here one of the corps' finest gives another marine a haircut.

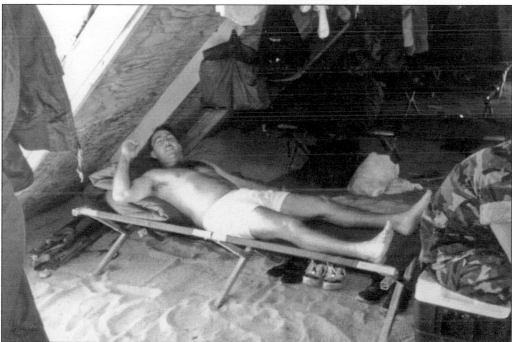

OLD A-FRAME SHELTERS. Camp Wilson, at the EAF, had a limited number of A-frames available for billeting during CAXs. They are simply aluminum-covered wood frames with sand floors, but they represent a substantial upgrade over tents, because they are much cooler. Here an anonymous CH-53 crew chief lies near the A-frame hatch to catch a breeze in the off-duty uniform of the day.

NEW QUONSET HUTS. Upon last inspection of the Camp Wilson area, dozens of these new Quonset Huts have been built, replacing the A-frames. With concrete floors and doors that close tightly, these facilities represent a quantum leap over their predecessors. The improvements are undoubtedly a direct result of the war in Iraq and Afghanistan, where conditions are even harsher than those found at Twentynine Palms and that have created myths such as camel spiders being the size of frisbees and running faster than the average marine.

EAF CONTROL TOWER COMPLEX. The short airfield for tactical support was undoubtedly conceived within moments after the first aircraft were used for military purposes. Almost immediately after World War I, marines found themselves in places like Haiti, Nicaragua, and the Dominican Republic carving airstrips out of dense jungle, on mountaintops, and on remote beaches. In World War II, the corps experimented with wooden planking for runways, and by the Korean War, pierced metal planks known as Marston Matting were used.

EAF's Mobile Radar and Communication. The idea for quickly deployed portable and mobile airfields was born in 1953 when the commandant of marines launched the corps into the development of a 1,000-foot portable airfield that could be constructed in five days. This was the airfield the marines constructed at Chu Lai; variations of it allow for arresting gear and JATO takeoffs or even a catapult. Lighting systems, crash equipment, navigation, radar and communications equipment, landing aids, and a portable control tower are all parts of the mobile concept. (Courtesy George Dietsch.)

EAF's CONTROL TOWER. During the Vietnam War, there was the famous story about General Westmoreland requiring an EAF at Chu Lai and asking each of his service chiefs how long it would take them to build one. The air force proudly announced they could do it in 20 months, the army laughed and said 12 months, and then the navy stepped in and said they could park an aircraft carrier near the beach. Marine General Krulak said, with a fat cigar in his mouth, that the Marine Corps could have the field ready in 30 days—and they did.

APPROACH END OF EAF RUNWAY. The EAF has a runway approximately 8,000 by 150 feet in size and is constructed of portable AM-2 matting covered with a nonskid coating. It is 2,051 feet above sea level and is classified as a military airfield requiring positive communication and permission prior to landing. Among its many features is a TAFDS (Tactical Airfield Fuel Dispensing System), consisting of very large, collapsible rubber fuel bladders for fuel storage with each holding 10,000 gallons and all the necessary pumps, filters, and hoses to hot-refuel aircraft.

AARF MARINES. The P-19 firefighting vehicle used by the Marine Corps is designed for operations in nuclear, biological, and chemical combat environments, as well as extreme weather conditions, and over varying terrain conditions found at EAFs where ever marines are. Aircraft Rescue-Fire Fighting and Recovery (AARF/R) marines are trained to fight aircraft fires and rescue pilots and aircrew from burning aircraft. Exploding fuel bladders and ordnance are a perpetual danger, making AARF/R one of the most demanding and dangerous jobs in the Marine Corps.

BELL "COBRA" HELICOPTERS. The AH-1 Cobra is an attack helicopter dating to the mid-1960s and the Vietnam War. The Marine Corps pioneered the helicopter-assault concept during the Korean War but discovered that slow-moving helicopters were vulnerable to ground fire. During the Vietnam War, the air-cavalry concept was expanded by the army, but helicopter losses to ground fire mounted. The attack helicopter was needed to protect troop-transport helicopters during assault missions.

COBRA USE IN VIETNAM. In June 1967, as the Vietnam War heated up, Bell Helicopters delivered the AH-1G Cobra to the U.S. Army. By 1973, Bell delivered 1,116 Cobras that flew over one million flight hours during the war. The Marine Corps obtained 38 AH-1G Cobra helicopters from the army in 1969 at the height of the Vietnam War. Initially, the Cobra's were assigned to UMO-2 but later transferred to HML-367. Everyone agreed the Cobra was an excellent weapons platform but earlier models were slow with a full load of weapons and fuel. The Marine Corps is currently looking at upgrading to the AH-1W Super Cobra with more powerful engines and four main rotor blades.

SLUGGISH COBRAS. Early model Cobras had a single engine and were relatively slow. Although advertised to fly 150 knots in a dive, the early Cobras were lucky to fly 100 knots on a hot day with a full bag of fuel and loaded with ordnance. This became a greater problem when the CH-53A/D Sea Stallion arrived in the inventory with a cruising speed of 170 knots. The Cobras could not keep up and the Sea Stallions did not want to slow down.

UPGRADING COBRAS. The Marine Corps has flown twin-engine Cobra's for a longtime and is transitioning to four-bladed Cobras that will increase airspeed, performance, and range, extending the already stellar design and performance of the Cobra decades into the future.

"BRONCO BUSTER." Another veteran of the skies over Twentynine Palms is the OV-10 Bronco. First delivered to Marine Squadron VMO-1 in February 1968, it was deployed to the Vietnam War soon afterward. The OV-10 had a compartment behind the cockpit for counter-insurgency para-ops, cargo, or two stretchers. Other missions flown by the Bronco were helicopter escorts, light-armed reconnaissance, and forward air-controller (FAC) duties. During the Vietnam War, OV-10 pilots were among the most courageous pilots flying.

SEA STALLION. Much of the mission of the large cargo/transport helicopters involves inserting and extracting marines to and from remote landing zones somewhere on the Twentynine Palms reservation. The marines disappear into the terrain and are usually not seen again by the helicopter crew until they call for resupply or extraction. The CH-53A was the first model Sea Stallion, and its early engines were limited in the high, hot terrain of Twentynine Palms. Later models of the Sea Stallion were much more capable.

FLYING OVER EMERSON (DRY) LAKE. Emerson Lake is a dry lake bed at Twentynine Palms used extensively by helicopter squadrons (here a CH53D Sea Stallion of HMH-363) for a variety of training cycles, from low-level navigation and terrain flight to night-vision goggle missions. During the day, practicing landings in a sandy desert landing zone is extremely challenging, because the helicopter usually becomes engulfed in a giant sandstorm just prior to touchdown, blinding the pilots. The sandstorm is created by the helicopter's rotor downwash.

SEA STALLIONS FLOWN BY RESERVES. This RH-53D Sea Stallion, of the HMH-769, sits on the ramp at the Twentynine Palms Expeditionary Air Field during one of many annual CAXs. It is unique in that it was only flown by the two Marine Corps' heavy lift reserve squadrons. The aircraft was originally designed for mine-sweeping duties in the navy and has larger engines, a beefed-up main transmission, and in-flight aerial refueling capability. Many pilots believe it to be the finest of all Sea Stallion aircraft, because it has excessive power and flies like a sports car.

ENORMOUS AIRCRAFT. The CH-53E Super Stallion is an enormous aircraft at 99.5 feet in length. Its maximum takeoff weight is 73,500 pounds with an external load and flies at 150 knots (172 miles per hour) with normal loads. At sea level, the helicopter can lift 32,000 pounds and travel 57.5 miles with that load and return. The CH-53E normally carries 37 passengers but can add seats to increase the passenger load to 55. The in-flight refueling system provides the capability for long-range missions deep into enemy territory for a variety of purposes.

WAITING FOR "MAN YOUR HELICOPTERS." Many of the Combined Arms Exercises include a large troop insert involving dozens of helicopters of all types in addition to overhead support from F/A-18 Hornets and AV-8 Harriers. These CH-53E Super Stallions are parked and awaiting the call to "man your helicopters." The Super Stallion has in-flight refueling capability, permitting extremely long-distance flights. Aerial refueling over the hot, turbulent skies of Twentynine Palms is one of the most challenging tasks asked of a helicopter pilot. The turbulence bounces the KC-130 tanker and the helicopter, making a connection from the refueling probe to the basket dangling from the KC-130 nearly impossible some days. The CH-53E flies with a minimum crew of three. (Courtesy Sikorsky Corporation.)

SUPER STALLION LIFTING A HOWITZER. The CH-53E Super Stallion is the Marine Corps heavy-lift workhorse and was specifically designed to transport much of the Marine Corps' heavier equipment. The ground crew "hooking up" the artillery must be very careful, because the Super Stallion builds up a significant charge of static electricity when flying, and that charge can knock a marine on his or her back if the aircraft is not properly grounded before hook up. (Photograph by Chief Warrant Officer Crow.)

SUPER STALLION LANDING FOR TROOP EXTRACT. A marine completing a mission or an exercise in the outback of Twentynine Palms usually has two options for returning to base camp where hot food and cold showers await: a long 20- to 30-mile bumpy ride that can take hours at slow speeds in the back of truck, baking in the hot sun, and choking on the dust and fumes from the convoy or a 15-minute ride in the back of a noisy but otherwise breezy and relatively comfortable helicopter. (Courtesy Sikorsky Corporation.)

SEA KNIGHT LANDING AT TWENTYNINE PALMS. The CH-46 Sea Knight is one of the Marine Corps' oldest airframes. First purchased in 1964 to meet medium-lift requirements during the Vietnam War, the CH-46 has served in all combat theaters and most peacetime environments since then. However, even with the upgraded engines and rotor blades, the CH-46 does not perform well in the high, hot deserts and mountains of Twentynine Palms. High-density altitude limitations often reduce the CH-46's effective payload by 75 percent. The OV-22 Osprey will soon replace the CH-46. (Courtesy FLAM.)

RAPPELLING FROM COPTER RAMP. This CH-46 Sea Knight, from HMM-764 Moonlighters, is working with ground units practicing rappelling from the helicopter's ramp.

SEA KNIGHT ON TROOP EXTRACTION DUTY. Grunts will attest that troop extraction, seen here and on the next page, is one of the best and worst experiences. They fall into the best experience category because the extraction usually follows a prolonged stay in the "boondocks" where bad chow, bad-tasting water, and foxhole living is the norm. They fall into the worst experience category because they are dangerous, dirty, wind blown from rotor wash, and chaotic.

THE OTHER SIDE OF EXTRACTION DUTY. However, the extractions are usually performed by pilots who either land too close and cover all the sweaty bodies with a thick coat of dirt from the rotor wash or too far away, making the grunts run a quarter-mile with their overloaded backpacks. The CH-46 is advertised to have a maximum gross takeoff weight of 24,000 pounds at sea level and a maximum airspeed of 145 knots. Earlier models rarely attained that performance level and never at Twentynine Palms with high-density altitude levels. Despite its limitations, the CH-46 has a long and notable record as a Marine Corps workhorse. (Courtesy FLAM.)

SEA KNIGHT CAPABILITIES. The CH-46, at the top, is capable of all-weather, day or night, night-vision goggle operations and is an assault transport aircraft that can insert or extract troops and provide supplies and ammunition. The Sea Knight is also used for medical evacuation missions, and one can almost always be found on standby at the Twentynine Palms MEDEVAC landing zone near the base hospital.

EXTERNAL LIFT OPERATIONS, CH-46E SEA KNIGHT. One of the primary missions of all military helicopters is performing external lift operations. A pendant and hook are extended below the helicopter's belly and attached to cargo on the ground by helicopter support team members. The crew chief of the HMM-764 Moonlighters, inside the helicopter looking down at the cargo through a hole in the helo's floor, gives the pilots directions as they are in the front and cannot see the men on the ground hooking up the cargo.

HELICOPTER DU JOUR. Many aircraft have flown in and out of Twentynine Palms since the marines took over in 1952, but few have flown as long and as often as the "Huey." Considered to be the most widely used helicopter in the world, it is flown in over 40 countries and more than 9,000 have been produced since the late 1950s. (Courtesy George Dietsch.)

VIETNAM WAR'S SIGNATURE "BIRD." The Huey first flew in 1956 and became famous during the Vietnam War. The UH-1N model Huey is a twin-piloted utility helicopter used in a variety of missions, including command and control, resupply, casualty evacuation, liaison and troop transport, assault support, and search and rescue among others. The UH-1N can carry six litter patients and one medical attendant. It can employ an external hoist and pick up external cargo as well as participate in special-operation missions. (Courtesy George Dietsch.)

FAST AND MANEUVERABLE. The A4 Sky Hawk pioneered the concept of the fast FAC. Until the late 1950s, airborne artillery and aircraft controllers flew over the battlefield in slow single-engine aircraft. The OV-10 Bronco improved the FAC's performance and longevity substantially, but it was also too slow and an easy target. The A4 Skyhawk had the airspeed and maneuverability to allow FACs to move around the battlefield and provide timely and accurate information to target planners while reducing their vulnerability to enemy gunners.

LAYING DOWN SMOKE. The skies over Twentynine Palms have seen countless real and experimental weapons come and go. This A4 Skyhawk is flying a low pass over ground forces, laying down a smoke screen, allowing them to maneuver or relocate under this cover. On a calm day with no winds, the smoke may linger for 30 minutes or more, but on a typical windy and turbulent Twentynine Palms day, the smoke could be gone in a few short minutes. (Courtesy FLAM.)

SKY HAWK SUPERIORITY. The A4 Sky Hawk emerged from the 1950s as one of the most versatile and capable attack aircraft of all time. It flew in the Marine Corps and Marine Corps Reserve from the 1950s to the mid-1990s, constantly being upgraded and improved. The aircraft is capable of carrying a variety of armament and is pictured here firing rockets. (Courtesy FLAM.)

A4 Sky Hawk. The A4 also served in the air forces of many foreign countries and continues to be flown into the 21st century. Here it is pictured dropping bombs onto the ranges at Twentynine Palms. The A4 was flown in the Marine Corps from the mid-1950s to the mid-1990s, continually being upgraded from the A4A model to the B, C, E, F, and M models. The last A4M was manufactured in 1979. (Courtesy FLAM.)

"GRAY GHOSTS." The F4 Phantom II of the VMFA-531 is a product of McDonnell Douglas that entered service in 1960 in the U.S. Navy and was adopted by the U.S. Air Force in 1963. It is an all-weather, supersonic, long-range bomber. As a very large and extremely heavy aircraft at a maximum takeoff weight of 60,000 pounds, the F4 is extremely fast, having set many records. It is capable of speeds of Mach 2.2 with an initial climb rate of over 41,000 feet per minute. Shortly after its introduction, the F4 Phantom II set a speed record of 1,606 miles per hour and an altitude record of 98,557 feet. The F4 can carry up to 18,650 pounds of weapons, including air-to-air and air-to-ground missiles and nuclear bombs. Early development of the F4 did not include an internal cannon or machine gun. It was thought at the time that guns were outdated and missiles would resolve air-to-air combat. Soon after the Vietnam War began, gun pods were added to the F4, giving it a much needed capability. (Courtesy FLAM.)

MARINE CORPS HARRIERS. If any aircraft was ever made for the EAF concept, it has to be the Harrier. A unique aircraft in every way, the Harrier is the only fixed-wing, short takeoff and landing aircraft in the world. The 1957, the P1127 model was based on a French design, adopted and improved by the British, and eventually acquire by the U.S. Marine Corps. Here an AV-8 Harrier from the VMA-513 Nightmares is taking off from the EAF runway. (Courtesy George Dietsch.)

ANOTHER AV-8 HARRIER. This one is flown by the VMA-211 Avengers. Upgrades have eventually yielded new engines and radar for the AV-8C Harrier II, and a forward-looking, infrared radar is on the horizon for the jet. (Courtesy FLAM.)

HORNET IN ACTION. An F/A-18 Hornet of VMFA-242 is depicted dropping ordnance. The F/A-18 was designed to combine the missions previously performed by the A4 Skyhawk, the F4 Phantom II, and the A6 Intruder in the Marine Corps plus the A7 Corsair in the U.S. Navy. In addition, the F/A-18 performs a variety of other missions, including air superiority, fighter escort, close and deep air support, reconnaissance, forward air control, and day and night strike capability. (Courtesy FLAM.)

HORNET CAPABILITIES. An F/A-18 Hornet of VMFA-312 takes off from EAF at Twentynine Palms. The F/A-18 performs extremely well there since it is capable of landing or taking off from the short decks of aircraft carriers. The F/A-18A became operational in 1983 and quickly earned a reputation for reliability and ease of maintenance. In 1987, the U.S. Navy began taking deliveries of the F/A-18C model with advanced missile systems capabilities and avionics. (Courtesy George Dietsch.)

A HORNET LANDS AT EAF. At the beginning of Desert Storm, two F/A-18s carrying four 2,000-pound bombs each shot down two Iraqi MiG jets and then continued their mission dropping bombs on target. The U.S. Navy and Marine Corps flew combat missions during Desert Storm continuously, establishing the F/A-18 as one of the most reliable and survivable jet aircraft ever built. (Courtesy George Dietsch.)

HERCULES POWER. This KC-130 Hercules powers up on the approach end of the Twentynine Palms EAF runway for departure. The KC-130 is one of the most enduring aircraft ever made and will probably take its place in history along side the DC-3. The F model Hercules was introduced in 1962. An extremely versatile platform, it can takeoff and land on short runways, in-flight refuel jets and helicopters, land in remote areas, serve as a ground refueling depot, and perform tactical insertion of troops among other missions. (Courtesy George Dietsch.)

Five

MILITARY UNITS AT TWENTYNINE PALMS

The Marine Corps acquired Twentynine Palms in 1952, eventually taking control of an area in excess of 930 square miles, which is approximately four-fifths the size of Rhode Island. In 1952, the base was christened Camp Detachment Marine Corps Training Center Twentynine Palms, California. On February 6, 1953, it was redesignated as Marine Corps Training Center and on February 1, 1957, the base was designated as a full-fledged Marine Corps Base (MCB). The commanding general of MCB Twentynine Palms was also the CG of Force Troops, 1st Marine Fleet Force, Pacific.

In the fall of 1957, the 1st Field Artillery Group (1st FAG) was created, consisting of the 1st Medium Antiaircraft Missile Battalion, 1st and 2nd Light Antiaircraft Missile Battalions, a detachment of the Force Service Regiment, D Company of the 7th Engineer Battalion, and the 5th Dental Company. During the late 1950s, the 1st FAG consisted of the 1st Heavy Artillery Rocket Battery with Honest John missiles; the 1st and 4th 155-mm Howitzer Batteries; the self-propelled 1st, 3rd, and 4th 155-mm Gun Batteries; the self-propelled 3rd and 4th 8-inch Howitzer Batteries; and a Headquarters Battery.

Over the years, the units serving at Twentynine Palms and the equipment have changed dramatically. Construction of an Expeditionary Air Field (EAF) was completed in 1976. On February 15, 1979, the base was renamed Marine Corps Air Ground Combat Center (MCAGCC), and on October 1, 2000, the base was renamed again to Marine Air Ground Task Force Training Command. The pace of training and activity at Twentynine Palms has increased dramatically over the years, and the base serves as a training hub for active-duty and reserve marines as well as members of the other armed forces. Today major commands include the 7th Marine Regiment, 1st Tank Battalion, 3rd Battalion 11th Marines, the 3rd LAR, CSSG-1, D Company 3rd Assault Amphibian Battalion, MWSS-374, VMU-1, MCCES, and the EAF.

TWENTYNINE PALMS LOGO. The Twentynine Palms logo attempts to capture much of what occurs there. Air, ground, artillery, tanks, amphibious vehicles, and much more represents the type of instruction that has made Twentynine Palms, perhaps, the best training facility in the U.S. armed forces. The Combined Arms Exercises (CAX) have been the hallmark of Twentynine Palms training since the late 1970s. However, modern world threats and terrorist tactics are changing the training dynamic, and there is no better place to train for new threats than at Twentynine Palms. The early CAXs at Twentynine Palms developed a scenario in a corridor of terrain several miles wide and 10 miles long, where Soviet forces are entrenched with various supporting arms and emplacements. Marines practice assaulting the Soviet forces and coordinating their own supporting arms and movement of forces. As the attack evolves, artillery and air assets destroy enemy positions, tanks close in, and troops advance. For unit leaders, command and control of this exercise provides invaluable training.

LOGO OF THE 7TH MARINES. The 7th Marines are one of the Marine Corps oldest and finest military units. Formed in 1917 during World War I, the unit was deactivated several times between conflicts but found itself in all the hot spots during World War II, the Korean War, the Vietnam War, and Desert Storm. The 7th Marines moved from Camp Pendleton to Twentynine Palms in 1990 but soon found themselves deploying to Iraq. Currently, the unit is the major Fleet Marine Force unit at Twentynine Palms, providing a historical reputation and leadership to all.

SEVENTH MARINES HEADQUARTERS BUILDING. During World War II, the 7th Marines joined the defense of Guadalcanal. For four long months, the regiment repelled and attacked the Japanese forces and their relentless banzai charges in an attempt to defeat the Americans and retake the island. These were the famous battles that produced hundreds of heroes, but among the better known are Manila John Basilone, Mitchell Paige, and Chesty Puller.

SEVENTH MARINES IN RECENT TIMES. In August 1991, 7th Marines was reorganized into Regimental Combat Team 7 (RCT-7) and deployed on Operation Restore Hope in Somalia. Over a five-month period, RCT-7 worked to provide humanitarian assistance and security for a war-torn nation on the verge of total collapse. Although the Marine Corps is well known for its combat prowess, the corps often assists those in need all over the world. During the aftermath of Hurricane Katrina, the Marine Corps deployed to New Orleans to help.

"Watch Dogs" Hangar. The VMU-1 Watch Dogs are hangared at Twentynine Palms main side for purposes of maintenance and ground training. During flight operations, the unit travels to the EAF, where it deploys unmanned aircraft at a remote site to avoid conflict and turbulence from other aircraft using the EAF. The services and capabilities provided by VMU-1 makes the squadron one of the busiest and most respected units in the Marine Corps.

Recently Formed Unit. The "V" in VMU-1 stands for fixed wing, the "M" for marines, the "U" for unmanned, and the numeral for the unit. The VMU-1 is one of the Marine Corps newest units, deploying unmanned, remotely piloted aircraft to perform reconnaissance, surveillance, and target-acquisition missions using the remotely piloted Pioneer Vehicle and the smaller ScanEagle. The creation and operation of this unit is in keeping with a long Marine Corps tradition of not only staying on the edge of the latest battlefield technology and tactics but in their development. In 1987, three of these systems were delivered to the Marine Corps. (Photograph by Gunnery Sergeant S. Arledge.)

DESERT STORM "PIONEER." The Pioneer performed with unprecedented success during Desert Storm, flying over 300 combat missions. The aircraft's accomplishments during the conflict include, but were not limited to, providing critical intelligence information concerning Iraqi troop, tank, and artillery placements and was recognized as the most important intelligence asset on the battlefield. The current RQ-2 Pioneer vehicle is 14 feet long, 3 feet high, has a 17-foot wingspan, and reaches speeds of 110 knots. The ScanEagle is smaller than the Pioneer II but is also yielding excellent intelligence. (Courtesy U.S. Navy.)

First Tank Battalion Logo. The 1st Tank Battalion is one of many Marine Corps units with a great history. Activated in November 1941, only weeks prior to the U.S. entry into World War II, the unit was ordered into the combat zone in the spring of 1942. Units of the 1st Tank Battalion were spread across the Pacific to support marines fighting in Samoa, New Zealand, Guadalcanal, and the Japanese Islands. They fought in the Korean War, the Vietnam War, Desert Storm, and today's battle to establish democracy in Iraq and fight terrorism.

TOP TANK BATTALION. The lst Tank Battalion is the Marine Corps' most highly decorated tank battalion. During Operation Desert Storm, the unit spearheaded the assault into Kuwait to free that country from Iraqi aggression. Shortly after their arrival at Kuwait International Airport, the efforts of the combined offensive destroyed all Iraqi forces. In 1992, the 1st Tank Battalion was transferred from Camp Pendleton to Twentynine Palms.

LOGO FOR "SEMPER FLEXIBILS." The 3rd Battalion 11th Marines was activated in 1943 during World War II and fought successfully throughout the march to Japan. In typical Marine Corps fashion, 3/11 participated in every major American conflict from World War II to Operation Iraqi Freedom. The battalion's motto, "Semper Flexibils," reflects its recent assignment to Iraq as a provisional military police battalion.

AMPHIBIOUS VEHICLES. In 1979, two platoons of Assault Amphibian Vehicles (formerly called AMTRAKS) arrived at Twentynine Palms to provide mechanized units in support of the Combined Arms Exercises (CAX). Additional platoons arrived later, and the units were redesignated. D Company continues to support CAXs, amphibious operations, fire support coordination, and application courses in addition to many other operations. D Company supports the 7th Marines and collateral projects, which includes the Advanced Assault Amphibian Vehicle (AAAV) testing and development program.

LOGO FOR "THE THUNDERING THIRD." The 3rd Battalion 4th Marines was activated in October 1925 in San Diego. In January 1927, the battalion departed for duty in Shanghai, China, which was a "hot spot" during the years prior to World War II because Japan and the U.S. had interest there, thus earning the coveted reputation as being part of the China marines who gained notoriety in the 1920s. At the onset of World War II, the unit was captured at Corregidor, enduring the Bataan March and imprisonment in Japanese POW camps. Over the ensuing decades, 3rd Battalion 4th Marines has traversed the world supporting combat actions against the enemies of democracy.

"WOLFPACK" LOGO. The much-traveled 3rd Light Armored Reconnaissance Battalion (3rd LAR) wears the Wolfpack logo.

GLOBE-TROTTING MARINES. The 3rd LAR began receiving Light Armored Vehicles (LAVs) in April 1984. Since then, the unit has relocated from Okinawa, Japan, to Twentynine Palms, Saudi Arabia, and Kuwait City. Then from Korea to the Philippines and Thailand to Somalia and back to Iraq and probably a few places not mentioned here. The LAV family of vehicles are highly mobile and are able to traverse land and water providing a range of combat options for commanders in the field.

"Rhinos" Logo. The EAF is under the control of the Commanding General 3rd Marine Aircraft Wing, and MWSS-374 has the responsibility for day-to-day operations. The EAF concept, to be able to quickly construct an airfield in remote places, allows marine squadrons and units to forward deploy its air assets to support the battle plan. MWSS-374, the Rhinos, feel their nickname represents their toughness and ability to perform in the harsh Twentynine Palms elements.

Unique "Rhinos." Marine Wing-Support Squadrons (MWSS) have evolved over the decades since World War II and Korea into the ultimate airfield construction and operation organization. There are no other units like them in the Marine Corps. They are composed of many different and unrelated types of elements such as a military police unit, a medical unit, a water-purification unit, carpentry and electrical construction units, and crash-fire-rescue units (now called aircraft rescue firefighting and recovery) and also have a variety of heavy-equipment operators.

CONSTRUCTION "RHINOS." The fundamental purpose of a Marine Wing Support Squadron is to deploy to a remote location and build an EAF as quickly as possible. This includes planning and logistics; engineering; soil preparation, grading, and laying the AM2 matting for runways and taxiways; setting up the portable fuel bladders and pumps, the arresting gear, the control tower, the navigation aids; and finally maybe adding some creature comforts for the troops.

FIREFIGHTING MARINES. The Aircraft Rescue Fire Fighting and Recovery Unit's primary mission is to ensure the rescue and safety of personnel involved in aircraft mishaps on the EAF or its immediate environment. This occasionally requires travel to the far corners of the 952-square-mile military base. ARFF/R vehicles are capable of traversing much of the back roads and rough terrain common to Twentynine Palms and delivering fire suppressants and emergency aid upon arrival.

EAF COMMANDS. The units operating the Twentynine Palms EAF have changed names, designations, and missions numerous times over the years. In 1977, MABS-11 Detachment operated the EAF. In 1979, MABS-11 Detachment was attached to MWSG-37 and was later renamed MWSG-37 Detachment Bravo in 1982. In 1988, MWSS-173 arrived from Hawaii to operate the EAF but was deactivated in 1993. Aviation Ground Support Element took over EAF operations until 1999, when it was redesignated MWSS-374.

CONTINUING EDUCATION. The Marine Corps Communication-Electronics School sign in front of the Twentynine Palms School welcomes nearly 6,500 students annually to attend courses that vary from 2 to 54 weeks in length. In 2006, MCCES partnered with the U.S. Army to create MCCES "E" University, placing many military courses on the internet to allow marines to advance their education anywhere they can find a computer.

HEADQUARTERS BUILDING. MCCES began its long history in 1932 as the "Pigeon and Flag Handler Platoon" back in the days when much communication was performed by carrier pigeons, signal flags, and signal mirrors. After many relocations and name changes, the unit landed at Twentynine Palms as the Communications-Electronics School Battalion. During 2005, the average MCCES student population was about 1,250 students who attended 44 different courses, which in turn produced 37 different military occupational specialties.

CARRIER PIGEON AIRPORT. During the early part of the 20th century, and for many centuries prior, battlefield communications often depended upon carrier pigeons. The Marine Corps' Pigeon and Flag Handler Platoon actually trained pigeons for delivering communications on the battlefield. This image of an early "pigeon airport" shows many of the birds arriving at their destination with communiqués tied to their feet.

Six

U.S. Navy at Twentynine Palms

The U.S. Navy plays an integral role in many aspects of Marine Corps operations and training as well as health care. Every Marine Corps installation has significant medical facilities on board to treat and maintain the health of marines. In addition to providing the corps with the entire panoply of health-care services, the navy provides combat corpsmen who keep an eye on marines during training cycles and join marines on the battlefield. Combat corpsmen are among the most respected individuals in any marine unit. Corpsmen have established a long and heroic heritage of bravery and self-sacrifice taking care of wounded marines in combat. The marines at Twentynine Palms also have a modern hospital facility called the Robert E. Bush Naval Hospital, which was named after Hospital Apprentice First Class R. E. Bush USN.

First Class Petty Officer Bush received the Medal of Honor for his heroic actions serving with the 5th Marines during World War II on Okinawa. During a battle, Bush attended to a wounded marine officer when Japanese soldiers overran his position. Bush emptied his pistol into the charging enemy soldiers and then grabbed a discarded carbine and continued firing, killing at least six enemy combatants despite receiving several serious wounds himself. Disregarding his own very serious injuries, he continued medical treatment on the wounded officer until they were safely evacuated. It was only then that he collapsed.

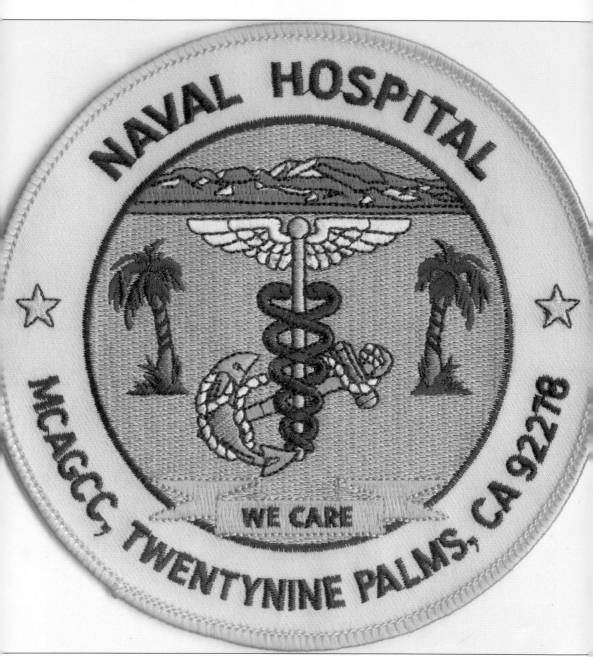

NAVAL HOSPITAL

MCAGCC, TWENTYNINE PALMS, CA 92278

WE CARE

U.S. Navy Patch. The Robert E. Bush Naval Hospital is a tenant command of the Marine Corps base at Twentynine Palms. The hospital is dedicated and staffed to provide medical care to marines and their families and to the retired community in the Twentynine Palms area. The hospital is accredited by the Joint Commission on Accreditation of Healthcare Organizations and received the 2003 Lead Agent's Award for "Best Military Treatment Facility of Southern California" as well as many other awards.

NAVY HOSPITAL MURAL. This large mural painted on an adjacent wall portrays the navy hospital logo and the Marine Corps emblem, illustrating the strong relationship between the two organizations.

NAVY'S DESERT HOSPITAL. Another view of the front entrance of the hospital includes a large anchor. Although serving well inland on a base in the Mojave Desert, naval personnel have their roots and heart on board a ship.

U.S. Navy Hospital Memorial. The front entrance to the Robert E. Burns Naval Hospital has several memorials depicting navy corpsmen rendering aid to marines fallen in combat. Here a corpsman holds a plasma bottle in one hand and a .45-caliber pistol in the other, illustrating the actions of the hospitals namesake on Okinawa in 1945. Parts of Hospital Apprentice First Class Burns's Medal of Honor citation reads as follows: "For conspicuous gallantry and intrepidity beyond the call of duty while serving with the First Marine Division on Okinawa, fearlessly braving the fury of artillery, mortar and machine-gun fire Bush unhesitatingly moved from one casualty to another to attend the wounded falling under the enemy's murderous barrages. While attending a wounded marine officer and providing plasma in one hand he had to draw his pistol with the other and fire into the enemy's ranks until the pistol was empty. Grabbing a discarded carbine he continued firing felling at least six enemy soldiers despite being wounded and losing an eye in the fire fight. After the fire fight he disregarded his own wounds and continued tending to the wounded Marine."

U.S. NAVY MEDICAL HERITAGE SERVING MARINE CORPS. This photograph shows a couple of wounded veterans of World War I and their favorite navy nurse. Marines have long heralded the care provided by navy nurses. Often near forward combat positions, these nurses have risked their lives to care for wounded marines and are well regarded.

DENTAL CORPS. Old-time military dentistry was much like medicinal practices of the day. Old battlefield doctors had one cure for every wound—amputation—and usually only had a hatchet and a saw in their medicine kit. Old battlefield dentists had one solution for all dental problems— pull it—often keeping only a pair of pliers and a wooden mallet in their bag of instruments. Times have changed, thank goodness, and modern military dentistry is as good as it gets. This image is of a mobile dental truck used in the Korean War.

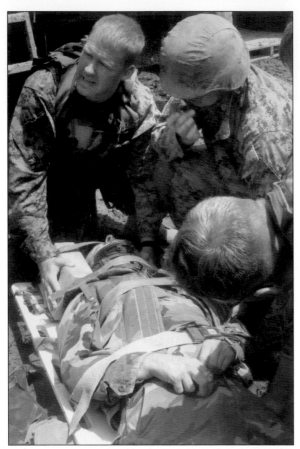

MODERN CORPSMAN. Modern navy corpsmen carry on the tradition of caring for wounded marines on and off the battlefield. With advances in technology and treatments, corpsmen are more valuable and proficient than ever and often perform just short of miracles when practicing their trade.

CHAPLAIN CORPS. The navy also provides a chaplain's corps that renders spiritual enlightenment and professional counseling to those in need. It is not uncommon for marines or family members of marines to encounter a variety of personal emergencies where chaplains and their professional staff often enter the picture. Chaplains from many religions serve in the navy, and among their many other duties, they perform religious services at the base chapel.

Seven

CITY OF
TWENTYNINE PALMS

The City of Twentynine Palms grew out of the grit and determination of early explorers, pioneers, prospectors, miners, and settlers. Creating a home or running a business in the desert, or merely surviving in the desert, can be listed among the great challenges of human endurance and perseverance. Amid the aridity, widely fluctuating temperatures, brutal winds, scorching sun, and unforgiving terrain, anything that has survived has withstood the test of time, including the Marine Corps. The pioneering spirit and toughness of the early Twentynine Palms settlers laid the foundation for every part of the community that followed.

In 1927, the homesteaders of Twentynine Palms built their own schoolhouse with donated land, money, material, and labor. It had eight students, but within only four years an additional room was necessary. By 1940, the school added a third room and had 90 students enrolled. The excess student body was often taught at private homes or other locations in town. The three-room schoolhouse met other social requirements and often served as a meeting place and a community center for things such as dances and even religious services.

The old schoolhouse served the community until the last classes were held in 1954. The building continued to be used by the Morongo Unified School District for office space and storage until 1990. At that time, the buildings were offered to the Twentynine Palms Historical Society. The society raised funds to relocate the schoolhouse to its current location near the Oasis of Mara. Since the relocation, the society has rehabilitated the old schoolrooms and added a gift shop, turning the building into a fine museum and local historical center. The windmill on the building works, and it has the distinction of being the oldest public building in use in the Morongo Basin.

The Twentynine Palms Historical Society was founded on April 26, 1982, and was incorporated on August 23, 1982, as a nonprofit public benefit corporation. It continues its original purpose of preserving and interpreting the historical heritage of the Twentynine Palms area through a variety of educational activities, including field trips, lectures, and a quarterly newsletter.

OASIS OF MARA. The Oasis of Mara, pronounced "Marrah" by the indigenous Chemehuevi Indians, is translated as "land of little water." When white explorers first discovered the oasis, there were several ponds, and water was so plentiful that the local Native Americans used it for irrigation and cattle grazing. The oasis was one of the few natural water sources in the Twentynine Palms area that made it a center of activity and survival for early residents. Dating the oasis is difficult, but anthropologists estimate humans have been using it for at least 11,000 years.

OASIS ADOBE. In 1878, an adobe hut was built at the oasis that served the many travelers, miners, settlers, and homesteaders who traveled, worked, or settled in the area. Conditions in the desert can be harsh, and protection from the heat, the wind, and the cold in any form was welcome. Historically, the oasis provided lifesaving water for various species of animals, including wild horses, bobcats, and dozens of birds. At least 13 reptile species have been identified at the oasis, including several types of snake. Encroachment by civilization has placed many species in danger.

STAGE LINE AT OASIS OF MARA. A stagecoach serviced the Twentynine Palms area, stopping at the oasis until made obsolete by automobiles in the early 20th century. (Courtesy TPHS.)

CITY MURALS—INDIAN HERITAGE. Over recent years, the City of Twentynine Palms has undertaken a project of painting large historical murals on the exterior walls of city buildings. It seems that nearly a dozen or more of these murals are spread throughout the city depicting significant historical events and people. This mural shows a day in the life of a Native American belonging to the Chemehuevi tribe in the mid-1800s, while a survey team encroaches upon their land.

GOLD MINING AT TWENTYNINE PALMS. During the initial rush to California to find gold, the Twentynine Palms area was ignored because conditions were difficult and water was scarce. However, by the late 1870s, prospectors found gold in the Twentynine Palms area. This area is a re-creation of an early gold mine located in the area.

REMNANTS OF GOLD RUSH. By the mid-1920s, much of the gold mining in the Twentynine Palms area had ended. The hills are littered with mine shafts, dirt piles, rotted timbers, and rusted equipment as a testament to the effort. This mural on the side of a building depicts the labor involved in early gold mining.

"THE FATHER OF TWENTYNINE PALMS." Dr. Luckie is credited with, if not putting Twentynine Palms on the map, at least expanding the population. After World War I, Dr. Luckie practiced medicine in Pasadena, and he was visited by many World War I veterans suffering respiratory problems from the poison gases used in Europe during the war. He began sending ailing veterans to Twentynine Palms to file homesteads hoping the clean, dry air would expedite their healing.

THE BAGLEYS. Frank and Helen Bagley arrived in Twentynine Palms in 1929 on Thanksgiving Day with their three sons. They filed a 160-acre homestead and began setting up shop and building their 18-by-18-foot home. Outside they installed a gas pump primarily for personal trips "down below" to Palm Springs. Eventually, as a result of running errands and picking up supplies for their neighbors, their building became a general store.

BAGLEY'S MARKET AND WATER TOWER. Frank Bagley's Market at Twentynine Palms became the center of activity and other businesses joined it. The Bagleys are thought of by many as early pioneers, if not the founders, as the glue that bonded the community together in the early days after World War I. Frank Bagley and his dog Skippy were usually found in front of the store helping friends and customers or simply socializing. Someone placed the "City Hall" sign on the Bagley Market water tower as a practical joke, and the prank eventually led to a *Ripley's Believe it or Not* citation as the smallest city hall in the world.

FLASH FLOOD MURAL. Desert communities are always in danger from harsh weather patterns, especially flash floods. The 1930s seemed to bring exceptionally harsh combinations of thunderstorms and snowstorms to Southern California. The homes, roads, and drainage in those days were much less equipped to handle the excesses than they are today, and a freak thunderstorm could become a community disaster.

MORE FLASH FLOODS. During the mid-1930s, and again in the late 1940s, thunderstorms and snowstorms inundated the Twentynine Palms area. The murals on city buildings illustrate not only the seriousness of flash flooding but also its impact on the town. Freak snowstorms are not as uncommon in the higher desert elevations as they are throughout most of Southern California.

SMITH FAMILY RANCH. In 1923, Bill Smith drove to Twentynine Palms in his Model T Ford and filed a homestead intent on developing a ranch. With his brother Harry, they drilled a well and provided water to their neighbors as well as a shower, swimming pool, and the shade from their Athol Trees, a welcome place to cool down during hot Twentynine Palms summers.

JOHNIE HASTIE. Johnie Hastie started his transportation business in 1937 and ran it successfully for many years. Hastie owned and operated the first motor stage line between the cities of Twentynine Palms and Banning, California. He converted a 1928 Chevrolet one-and-a-half-ton truck, with a four-cylinder engine and top speed of 25 miles per hour, into a bus. The vehicle was heated by a wood stove in the winter.

STAGE STUBS. Depicted are ticket stubs for the Hastie Motor Stage Line. At 25 miles per hour, the journey from Twentynine Palms to Riverside could have taken days.

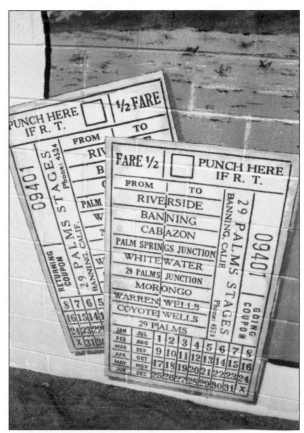

JACK CONES, "THE FLYING SHERIFF." Orville Jackson Cones, or "Cactus Jack," could make a tin can dance in the sand with his gun. Arriving in Twentynine Palms in 1929, Cones became the constable in 1932, holding the position for the next 28 years. The Flying Sheriff piloted a J-3 Piper Cub from his private airfield and patrolled over 2,800 square miles of rugged desert searching for wrongdoers and landing on dirt roads to help stranded travelers. Larger than life, Cactus Jack earned his place in Twentynine Palms folklore.

SEND IN THE MARINES. Since 1952, when the marines landed in Twentynine Palms, the corps has played a large part in the development of the area and has developed a great relationship with the citizens and local government. Part of the city's historic mural program was dedicated to the Marine Corps after Desert Storm, manifesting the city's respect for marines.

LITTLE CHURCH OF THE DESERT. A groundbreaking ceremony for the Little Church of the Desert was held on November 3, 1935. However, as the nation emerged from the Great Depression, fundraising was slow. By February 1936, pledges, not cash in hand, totaled $583.50. A radio show on KMTR Los Angeles sparked interest in the church project and many World War I veterans rallied for the cause, making substantial donations. On September 1, 1940, the first service was held.

THE HISTORIC PLAZA. The Plaza, originally called Supply Place, predates modern shopping centers, as it originated in 1927 and was remodeled in 1936. Much of the business in Twentynine Palms in the 1930s involved the local mining industry, but with the advent of World War II in 1941 and influx of military personnel, the city grew substantially. This laid the foundation for a modern city and marketplace to develop.

125

OLD SCHOOLHOUSE AND MUSEUM. During the mid-1920s, the homesteaders of Twentynine Palms were denied funds by San Bernardino County to build their first school. The residents, in typical fashion, would not be denied, and with some donated land, a little money, materials, and a lot of sweat, they built their own one-room schoolhouse. Within four years, another room was added, and by 1940, they had three rooms and 90 students. Eventually, the schoolhouse served the entire Morongo Basin.

ANOTHER OLD SCHOOLHOUSE AND MUSEUM VIEW. In 1990, the building was offered to the Twentynine Palms Historical Society. The society began what evolved into a very successful fund-raising campaign, resulting in the 3,000-square-foot schoolhouse being relocated on April 4, 1992, nearly 2 miles away to a site owned by the society near the Oasis of Mara and the Twentynine Palms Inn. The school was then refurbished and opened as a museum with a gift shop. It has a research library dedicated to the preservation of Twentynine Palms history, and it is the oldest public building in the Morongo Basin.

OLD SCHOOLHOUSE AND MUSEUM. This old schoolhouse and classroom illustrate how so much was accomplished with so little. It begs the question, "Why are we doing so poorly in today's schools spending billions of dollars?" The Twentynine Palms School House and Museum is open to the public.

ACROSS AMERICA, PEOPLE ARE DISCOVERING SOMETHING WONDERFUL. *THEIR* HERITAGE.

Arcadia Publishing is the leading local history publisher in the United States. With more than 3,000 titles in print and hundreds of new titles released every year, Arcadia has extensive specialized experience chronicling the history of communities and celebrating America's hidden stories, bringing to life the people, places, and events from the past. To discover the history of other communities across the nation, please visit:

www.arcadiapublishing.com

Customized search tools allow you to find regional history books about the town where you grew up, the cities where your friends and family live, the town where your parents met, or even that retirement spot you've been dreaming about.